Jargon 92

BOTH

PAUL METCALF

BOTH

THE JARGON SOCIETY
1982

This project is supported by a grant
from the *National Endowment for the Arts* in Washington, D.C.,
a Federal agency created by Act of Congress in 1965.

Manufactured in the United States of America by
Heritage Printers, Inc., Charlotte, North Carolina

Designed by Fielding Dawson & Jonathan Williams.
Credit and thanks are due to the collections of the New York
Public Library for the photograph of Poe, and to the
Library of Congress for the photograph of Booth.

Distributed by
Inland Book Company
22 Hemingway Avenue
East Haven, Connecticut 06512
Telephone: (203) 467–4257

Travelling Light (UK & Europe)
62 West Hill,
London SW18 1RU, England

CONTENTS

"He was so much against slavery that he had begun to include prose and poetry in the same book, so that there would be no arbitrary boundaries between them."

— Ishmael Reed

POE

David Poe, Jr., a letter to his cousin, eighteen 0 nine:

"Sir, *You* promised *me* on your honor to meet me at the Mansion house on the 23d - *I* promise *you* on *my* word of honor that if you will lend me 30, 20, 15 or even 10$ I will *remit* it to you *immediately* on my arrival in Baltimore. Be assured I will keep *my* promise at least as well as you did yours and that nothing but extreme distress would have *forc'd* me to make this application - Your answer by the bearer will prove whether I yet have 'favour in your eyes' or whether I am to be despised by (as I understand) a rich relation because when a *wild boy* I join'd a profession when I then thought and now think an honorable one. But which I would most willingly quit tomorrow if it gave satisfaction to your family provided I could do *any thing* else that would give bread to mine - Yr. Politeness will no doubt enduce you to answer this note from Yrs &c

D. POE JR."

. . . left a career in the law, to follow the disreputable profession of acting . . .

. . . married an actress, Elizabeth Hopkins (nee Arnold), "a lovely little creature" "with the aura of unreality which the stage imparts" . . .

. . . raised a family, trouped the eastern seaboard, in six years on the stage played one hundred and thirty-seven roles . . .

. . . but was less than a successful actor, suffering as he did from "sudden indispositions" which sent him to the stage staggering . . .

. . . was reviewed once as "sur un POE de chambre" . . .

. . . left his young wife, disappeared . . .

. . . and she trouped alone, with the infants . . .

. . . she was delicate, tubercular, and in Richmond, in her boarding house room . . . in the presence of her young son Edgar, who was less than three years old . . . she spit blood, and died . . .

*   *   *

. . . the child remembered:

"The sight of blood inflamed its anger into phrensy" and the garments of the men who came to cart his mother away were

"*nigrum nigrius nigro*"

*   *   *

To attain the hypnagogic state, between sleep and reason, between death and life . . .

> "The boundaries which divide Life from Death are at best shadowy and vague."

To depart the life of this earth, and to be interred - but still alive!

> "It may be asserted, without hesitation, that *no* event is so terribly well adapted to inspire the supremeness of bodily and of mental distress, as is burial before death. The unendurable oppression of the lungs - the stifling fumes of the damp earth - the clinging to the death garments - the rigid embrace of the narrow house - the blackness of the absolute Night - the silence like a sea that overwhelms . . . "

To become one "whose pleasure lies in arousing and bearing anxiety, through loss of balance, stability and contact with firm earth."

*   *   *

The infant Edgar, adopted by the John Allans of Richmond, was educated in England and Virginia, enrolled in the University at Charlottesville . . .

> (" . . . debts were accummulated, and money borrowed of Jews in Charlottesville at extravagant interest . . . It was then that I became dissolute, for how could it be otherwise?")

enlisted in the army,
was appointed to West Point
. . . and court-martialled

lived in Baltimore with his aunt Mrs. Clemm
. . . was disowned by Allan . . .
grubbed a meager literary living

. . . 1835, married his first cousin Virginia Clemm
(age 14)
and, with her mother,
set up housekeeping:

Eddie, Sissy and Muddy

Young Virginia: slender, delicate, prone to weakness of the lungs . . .

". . . a picture of a young girl just ripening into womanhood."

"The portrait, I have already said, was that of a young girl. It was a mere head and shoulders . . . The arms, the bosom, and even the ends of the radiant hair melted imperceptibly into the vague yet deep shadow which formed the background of the whole."

"In time the crimson spot settled steadily upon the cheek, and the blue veins upon the pale forehead became prominent; and, one instant, my nature melted into pity, but, in the next, I met the glance of her meaning eyes, and then my soul sickened and became giddy with the giddiness of one who gazed into some dreary and unfathomable abyss."

*   *   *

To attain the spirit's outer world . . .

" . . a gay and motley train of rhapsodical and immethodical thought."

"*All* that we see or seem
Is but a dream within a dream."

"Would to God I could awaken

For I dream I know not how . . ."

"And all my days are trances . . ."

*   *   *

"I really believe that I have been mad . . ."

*   *   *

"At no period of my life was I ever what men call intemperate. I never was in the *habit* of intoxication. I never drank drams, &c. But, for a brief period, while I resided in Richmond, and edited the *Messenger* I certainly did give way, at long intervals, to the temptation held out on all sides by the spirit of Southern conviviality. My sensitive temperament could not stand an excitement which was an everyday matter to my companions. In short, it sometimes happened that I was completely intoxicated."

". . . the occasional use of *cider*, with the hope of relieving a nervous attack."

"During these fits of absolute uncon-
sciousness I drank, God only knows
how often or how much."

                    "All was hallucination, arising from an
                    attack which I had never before experi-
                    enced - an attack of mania-a-potu."

("No man is safe who drinks before
breakfast!")

                    "I call God to witness that I have never
                    loved dissipation . . ."

"I have been taken to prison once since
I came here for getting drunk . . ."

                    "I have fought the enemy manfully . . ."

"I am resolved not to touch a drop as
long as I live."

                    "I am done forever with drink."

"My *habits* are rigorously abstemious
and I omit nothing of the natural regi-
men, requisite for health: - i.e. - I rise
early, eat moderately, drink nothing but
water . . ."

> ". . . the causes which maddened me to
> the drinking point are no more, and I
> am done drinking forever."

"Will you be kind enough to put the
best possible interpretation upon my be-
havior in N-York? You must have con-
ceived a *queer* idea of me - but the simple
truth is that Wallace would insist upon
the juleps, and I knew not what I was
either doing or saying."

> ". . . humming-stuff . . ."

> ("Poe is not in Richmond. He remained
> here about 3 weeks, horribly drunk and
> discoursing 'Eureka' every night to the
> audiences of the Bar Rooms.")

*   *   *

"Happiness is [Man's] purpose. The sources of that, he may be told, are in himself - but his eye will fix on the external means, and these he will labor to obtain. Foremost among these, and the equivalent which is to purchase all the rest, is property. At this all men aim . . ."

". . . to combine the ideas of an agility astounding, a strength superhuman, a ferocity brutal, a butchery without motive, a *grotesquerie* in horror absolutely alien from humanity, and a voice foreign in tone to the ears of men of many nations, and devoid of all distinct or intelligible syllabification."

"There were a great many women and children, the former not altogether wanting in what might be termed personal beauty. They were straight, tall, and well formed, with a grace and freedom of carriage not to be found in civilized society. Their lips, however, like those of the men, were thick and clumsy . . ."

"In the calm, and, as we would call it, the healthful condition of the public mind . . . we find each quietly enjoying his own property,

"Each animal, if you will take the pains to observe, is following, very quietly, in the wake of its master. Some few, to be sure, are led with

and permitting to others the quiet enjoyment of theirs . . . Peace reigns, the arts flourish, science extends her discoveries, and man, and the sources of his enjoyments, are multiplied."

a rope about the neck, but these are chiefly the lesser or timid species. The lion, the tiger, and the leopard are entirely without restraint. They have been trained without difficulty to their present profession, and attend upon their respective owners in the capacity of *valets-de-chambre*."

"A very short while sufficed to prove that this apparent kindness of disposition was only the result of a deeply laid plan for our destruction, and that the islanders for whom we entertained such inordinate feelings of esteem, were among the most barbarous, subtle, and blood-thirsty wretches that ever contaminated the face of the globe."

"Fifty years ago, in France, this eccentric comet, 'public sentiment', was in its opposite node . . . it should be remembered now, that in that war against property, the

"It was quite evident that they had never before seen any of the white race - from whose complexion, indeed, they appeared to recoil."

first object of attack was property in slaves. . ."

"We speak of the moral influences flowing from the relation of master and slave, and the moral feelings engendered and cultivated by it."

". . . unless we take into consideration the peculiar character (I may say the peculiar nature) of the negro."

"Let us reason upon it as we may, there is certainly a power, in causes inscrutable to us, which works essential changes in the different races of animals. . . . The color of the negro no man can deny, and therefore it was but the other day, that they who will believe nothing they cannot account for, made this manifest fact an authority for

"In truth, from everything I could see of these wretches, they appeared to be the most wicked, hypocritical, vindictive, blood-thirsty, and altogether fiendish race of men upon the face of the globe."

"Their complexion a jet black, with thick and long wooly hair. They were clothed in skins of an unknown black animal, shaggy and silky . . ."

"The bottoms of the canoes were full of black stones . . ."

". . . a black albatross . . ."

". . . black gannets . . ."

". . . brown celery . . ."

". . . blackfish . . ."

denying the truth of holy writ. Then comes the opposite extreme - they are, like ourselves, the sons of Adam, and must therefore, have like passions and wants and feelings and tempers in all respects. This, we deny . . ."

"Our theory is a short one. It was the will of God it should be so. But the means - how was this affected? We will give the answer to anyone who will develop the causes which might and should have blackened the negro's skin and crisped his hair into wool."

". . . a species of bittern, with jet black and grizzly plumage . . ."

". . . a very black and shining granite . . ."

". . . he who is taught to call the little negro 'his', in this sense and *because he loves him*, shall love him *because he is his*."

"The marl was also black; indeed, we noticed no light colored substances of any kind upon the island."

"He . . . made use of only idiotic gesticulations, such as raising with his forefinger the upper lip, and displaying the teeth which lay beneath it. These were black."

"Nothing is wanting but manly discussion to convince our own people at least, that in continuing to command the services of their slaves, they violate no law divine or human . . ."

"We noticed also several animals . . . covered with a black wool."

"Nature had endowed him with no neck, and had placed his ankles (as is usual with that race) in the middle of the upper portion of the feet."

"Seizing him furiously by the wool with both hands, I tore out a vast quantity of black, and crisp, and curling material, and tossed it from me with every manifestation of disdain."

*   *   *

Virginia Clemm Poe: slender, delicate, with a tendency toward weakness of the lungs . . .

"She was a good girl, and told me very sweet-
ly that I might have her (plum and all) . . .

(The pendulum, "massy and
heavy, tapering", swinging to the
circular pit . . .)

". . . but the fires were not of Eros, and bitter
and tormenting to my spirit was the gradual
conviction that I could in no manner define
their unusual meaning, or regulate their
vague intensity . . ."

"The forehead was high, and very pale, and singularly
placid; and the once jetty hair fell partially over it, and
overshadowed the hollow temples with innumerable
ringlets, now of a vivid yellow, and jarring discordant-
ly, in their fantastic character, with the reigning melan-
choly of the countenance. The eyes were lifeless, and
lustreless, and seemingly pupilless, and I shrank invol-
untarily from their glassy stare to the contemplation of
the thin and shrunken lips. They parted; and in a smile
of peculiar meaning, *the teeth* of the changed Berenice
disclosed themselves slowly to my view . . . for these I
longed with frenzied desire."

(But the pendulum, swinging:
"Could I resist its glow? or if even
that, could I withstand its pressure?")

1842, Edgar Allan Poe was at last out of debt. He was employed, and
content with home and family: Eddie, Sissie and Muddy. "In the evening, after the plentiful dinner that Mrs. Clemm now could supply
without stint, the occupants of the little clapboard house were happy
together. Edgar would play the flute, and Virginia would sing to her
harp."

But, early that year: "Suddenly Virginia's
voice broke and died: blood streamed from
her throat."

She lay shivering in bed, Eddie's old army
coat thrown over her - Catarina, the family
cat, draped around her throat.

"But at length, as the labor drew nearer to its conclusion, there were
admitted none into the turret; for the painter had grown wild with the
ardor of his work, and turned his eyes from the canvas rarely, even to
regard the countenance of his wife. And he *would* not see that the tints
which he spread upon the canvas were drawn from the cheeks of her
who sat beside him. And when many weeks had passed, and but little
remained to do, save one brush upon the mouth and one tint upon the

eye, the spirit of the lady again flickered up as the flame within the socket of the lamp. And then the brush was given, and then the tint was placed; and, for one moment, the painter stood entranced before the work which he had wrought; but in the next, while he yet gazed, he grew tremulous and very pallid, and aghast, and crying with a loud voice, 'This is indeed *Life* itself!' turned suddenly to regard his be-loved: - *She was dead!*"

*   *   *

"... it is clear that a poem now written will be poetic in the exact ratio of its dispassion. A passionate poem is a contradiction in terms."

"[The poet] recognizes the ambrosia which nourishes his soul, in the bright orbs that shine in Heaven - in the volutes of the flower - in the clustering of low shrubberies - in the waving of the grain-fields - in the slanting of tall, Eastern trees - in the blue distance of moun-tains - in the grouping of clouds - in the twinkling of half-hidden brooks - in the gleaming of silver rivers - in the repose of sequestered lakes - in the star-mirroring depths of lonely wells. He perceives it in the songs of birds - in the harp of AEolus - in the sighing of the night-wind - in the repining voice of the forest - in the surf that complains to the shore - in the fresh breath of the woods - in the scent of the violet - in the volup-tuous perfume of the hyacinth - in the suggestive odor that comes to him, at eventide, from far-distant, undiscovered islands, over dim oceans, illimitable and unexplored."

"With the *passions* of mankind - although [a poem] may modify them greatly - although it may exalt, or inflame, or purify, or control them - it would require little ingenuity to prove that it has no inevitable, and indeed no necessary co-existence."

*   *   *

". . . Tellmenow Isitsöornot . . ."

"Most of them [the stories] were *intended* for half banter, half satire - although I might not have fully acknowledged this to be their aim even to myself."

"*The Atlantic has been actually crossed in a Balloon*! and this too without difficulty - without any great apparent danger - with thorough control of the machine - and in the inconceivably brief period of seventy-five hours from shore to shore!"

("Some few persons believe it - but *I* do not - and don't you. P.S. 'The Valdemar Case' was a hoax, of course.")

("Of course, there is not one word of truth in it from beginning to end . . . please *do not let out the secret*.")

. . . filled his stories with spurious quotations from foreign languages
. . . "makes quotations from the German, but he can't read a word of
the language."

. . . codes, ciphers and anagrams . . . acrostics, hieroglyphics, the
kabbala . . .

"I believe that demons take advantage of the night to mislead the
unwary - although you know, I don't believe in them."

". . . Tellmenow Isitsöornot . . ."

*   *   *

Worried about his appearance:

"I have been invited out a great deal - but could seldom go, on account
of not having a dress coat."

"My clothes are *so horrible* . . ."

Cultivated his moustache - the mark of the actor - "that was to become his trademark . . ."

> (until, near the end (1849), "Poe, pale and
> haggard, burst into John Sartain's office. He

begged Sartain to protect him from two men who, he said, were going to kill him. They had followed him on the train, but he had got off and returned to Philadelphia to avoid them. He insisted that Sartain cut off his moustache, so he could not be recognized . . .")

"His voice, I remember, was very pleasant in its tone and well modulated, almost rhythmical" . . . "he spoke with great precision" . . . "his voice seemed attenuated to the finest golden thread; the audience became hushed, and, as it were, breathless; there seemed no life in the hall but his; and every syllable was accentuated with such delicacy, and sustained with such sweetness, as I have never heard equally by other lips . . . I felt that we had been under the spell of some wizard" . . . "he seems to have chanted his verses instead of reading them in the ordinary sense" . . . "His voice was rich, his enunciation clear, and he read poems with a dramatic, almost histrionic power" . . .

Mrs. Clarke, who heard him read in Richmond, remembered the richness and mellowness and sweetness of Poe's voice, noting a resemblance to that of the actor Edwin Booth . . .

*   *   *

Margaret Fuller thought "he always seemed shrouded in an assumed character."

. . . actor and character, role and player, interfused, the other become his own, his own another . . .

Performing out of shyness: the theater - self-exhibition - the final retreat of the secretive . . .

"Richmond & the U. States were too narrow a sphere & the world shall be my theatre - "

*   *   *

Accused just about everyone, particularly Longfellow, of plagiarism . . .

("I am particularly anxious for a paper on . . . the subject of the Laws of Libel in regard to Literary Criticism . . .")

(accused Fenimore Cooper of "mental leprosy")

. . . wrote a book, *The Conchologist's Text Book*, which was a paraphrase of another's original . . .

". . . and the more you put in your book that
is not your own, why the better your book
will be: - but be cautious and steal with an
air."

*   *   *

*"Pure gold can be made at will, and very readily from lead in con-
nection with certain other substances . . ."*

John Sartain: "I asked him how he came to be in Moyamensing Prison, and he said he has been suspected of trying to pass a fifty-dollar
counterfeit note . . ."

*   *   *

". . . Tellmenow Isitsöornot . . ."

. . . to banish uncertainty, to interfuse, to blend . . .

. . . to marry one's cousin, to tell tales of incest . . .

. . . at various times gave his date of birth as 1809, 1811, 1813 . . .
at 37, called himself 33 . . .

. . . enlisted in the army as Edgar A. Perry, at other times became Henri le Rennet, Edward S. T. Grey, E. S. T. Grey Esqre., and Thaddeus K. Peasley . . .

*   *   *

Poe, the actor, playing his role, and Edgar, watching him play . . .

(Gertrude Stein: "I said and I said it well I said an actor sees what he says. Now think a little how he looks and how he hears what he says. He sees what he says.")

"The orange ray of the spectrum and the buzz of the gnat . . . affect me with nearly similar sensations."

*   *   *

"but I am still *very* unwell . . ."

"I am getting better, however, although slowly, and shall get *well*."

"I am still dreadfully unwell . . ."

("...congestion of the brain...")

Mrs. Shew: "I made my diagnosis, and went to the great Dr. Mott with it; I told him that at best, when Mr. Poe was well, his pulse beat only ten regular beats, after which it suspended, or intermitted (as doctors say). I decided that in his best health he had lesion of one side of the brain..."

On his deathbed: "... tremor of the limbs ... a busy but not violent or active delirium - constant talking - and vacant converse with spectral and imaginary objects on the walls ... a violent delirium, resisting the efforts of two nurses to keep him in bed ..."

... died - October 7, 1849 - of "chronic inflammation of the meninges."

*   *   *

In 1860 - long after Poe's burial in an unmarked grave - Judge Neilson Poe ordered a marble slab, properly inscribed. "It was lying in the yard with other monuments ready for delivery when a train of the Northern Central Railroad accidentally jumped the track and, of all slabs, shattered Poe's beyond repair."

"It was not until a quarter of a century after Poe's death that a group of Baltimore schoolteachers, aided by the citizenry, succeeded in raising enough money to honor the poet with a monument, and commissioned Sir Moses Ezekiel to execute it . . . The sculptor had finished his clay model and had sent it to the foundry to be cast into bronze when it was destroyed by fire."

"He modeled it for the second time, only to have an earthquake demolish it, together with the studio that housed it."

"The third time Sir Moses managed to get it cast before another intervention."

WATERWORLD

The Indian tribes of the Canadian Plains believed that all buffalo emerged from under a lake, and however recklessly the white man might slaughter, they would never be exterminated . . .

According to the Hopi, all bodies of water are parts of one great ocean underlying the earth . . . the springs are mere openings, or *eyes*, as the Spanish call them, peering through the earth crust, out of the water. world.

*   *   *

Adam Seaborn:

"In the year 1817, I projected a voyage of discovery, in the hope of finding a passage to a new and untried world. I flattered myself that I should open the way to new fields for the enterprise of my fellow-citizens, supply new sources of wealth, fresh food for curiosity, and additional means of enjoyment; objects of vast importance, since the resources of the known world have been exhausted by research, its wealth monopolized, its wonders of curiosity explored, its every thing investigated and understood!"

"I remembered the misfortune of the discoverer SINDBAD, whose ship, when he approached the magnetic mountain, fell to pieces, in consequence of the iron being all drawn out of it. To guard against a similar disaster, I fastened my vessel first with tree-nails, and then throughout with copper bolts firmly rivetted and clenched."

"Confident that, with this vessel, I could reach any place to which there was a passage by water, whether on the external or internal world, I named her the EXPLORER."

"On the 4th of September, we entered the harbour of West Point, Falkland Islands. Here I had determined to pass a month for the benefit of my health, which a short passage by water had not completely restored, from the debility occasioned by the vexations and anxieties of business in those retrograde times, and the pernicious habits of living, common among civilized men, upon food rendered palateable by a skilful admixture of poisons."

"I concurred in the opinion published by Capt. Symmes, that seals, whales, and mackerel, come from the internal world through the openings at the poles; and was aware of the fact, that the nearer we approach these openings, the more abundant do we find seals and whales."

earth opening, polar cleft,
source and passage of earth's
unending watery abundance!

birth-channel of whales and seals:
southern polar orifice

"This will give the polar region seven months constant day, with a continual stream of light and heat pouring upon the same spot, without any interval of night to cool the earth and air. I think if we can but find our way to the polar region, we shall be in much more danger of being roasted alive, than of being frozen to death."

erogenous!

"Slim: 'How will you justify yourself to the world, to our families, or to your own conscience, if we should, after effecting a passage through this 'icy hoop' you speak of, find it closed against our return, and be thus forever lost to our wives, our children, and society?' A plague upon your lean carcass, thought I . . . I could not tell him of my belief of open poles, affording a practicable passage to the internal world, and of my confident expectations of finding comfortable winter quarters inside; for he would take that as evidence of my being insane . . ."

"I edged away to the eastward, intending to keep near the ice, and hauled to the southward, when a clear sea would permit. The first day, we kept the 'blink of the ice'(*) in sight, and found it to trend nearly East and West."

"After a comfortable meal, and a sound nap of four hours, I descended the precipice to ascertain whether the river was an arm of the sea, or a fresh water stream. It proved to be pure potable water, and the existence of a continent near the south pole, was thus established."

"I was now convinced of the correctness of Capt. Symmes's theory, and of the practicability of sailing into the globe at the south pole, and returning home by way of the north pole, if no land intervened to obstruct the passage."

> an open passage,
> a clear sail,
> into earth internal!

"Having anchored the Explorer in a safe situation, I landed with a boat's crew at one of the open spaces, to examine the productions of the land, and see if I could discover any indications of inhabitants. I found the timber to be mostly different from that which I was acquainted with, excepting a species of fir resembling our spruce. . . . All fears of the consequence of wintering in this region were now done away. Where trees could live, I could live."

(*) an arch formed upon the clouds by the reflection of light from the packed ice.

the mound of delight

is piligerous!

". . . I was well aware that when they (the crew) would suppose we were sailing northward on the other side of the globe, we should in fact be sailing directly into it through the opening."

a song,

a geode,

to earth penetrated!

"I, Adam Seaborn, mariner, a citizen of the United States of America, did, on the 5th day of November, Anno Domini one thousand eight hundred and seventeen, first see and discover this southern continent, a part of which was between 78° and 84° south latitude, and stretching to the N.W., S.E., and S.W., beyond my knowledge; which land having never before been seen by any civilized people, and having been occupied for the full term of eighteen days by citizens of the said United States, whether it should prove to be in possession of any other people or not, provided they were not *Christians*, was and of right ought to be the sole property of the said people of the United States, by right of discovery and occupancy, according to the usages of Christian nations."

("I had it engraved on a plate of sheathing copper, with a spread eagle at the top, and at the bottom a bank, with 100 dollar bills tumbling out

of the doors and windows, to denote the amazing quantity and solidi-
ty of the wealth of my country.")

"I was perfectly aware that if the poles were open, of which I had no
doubt, we must . . . on turning the edge of the opening have a verti-
cal sun, an equal division of day and night, and all the phenomena of
the equator."

"The compass was now of no manner of use; the card turned round
and round on the slightest agitation of the box, and the needle pointed
sometimes one way and sometimes another, changing its position every
five minutes. . . . My best seamen appeared confounded . . . and a de-
gree of alarm pervaded the whole ship's company."

"We had a regular recurrence of day and night, though the latter was
very short, which I knew was occasioned by the rays of the sun being
obstructed by the rim of the earth, when the external side of the part
we were on turned towards the sun."

"I walked the deck all night, and was very impatient for the morning
of that day which was to disclose to me the wonders of the internal
world."

     sliding,
     sliding,

"I named this island, which was in 81° 20′ internal south latitude, Token Island, considering its discovery as a token or premonition of some great things to come."

sliding . . . *in*!

"I found the latitude this day, carefully computed from the sun's altitude, with due allowance for refraction, to be 65° 17′ south internal."

"My imagination became fired with enthusiasm, and my heart elated with pride. I was about to secure to my name a conspicuous and imperishable place on the tablets of History, and a niche of the first order in the temple of Fame. I moved like one who trod air; for whose achievements had equalled mine? The voyage of Columbus was but an excursion on a fish pond, and his discoveries, compared with mine, were but trifles . . . His was the discovery of a continent, mine of a new World!"

penetrating, invading,
violating
the gentle virgin,
Earth

"The soft reflected light of the sun, which was now no longer directly visible, gave a pleasing mellowness to the scene, that was inexpressibly agreeable, being about midway between a bright moonlight and clear sunshine. I had great cause to admire the wonderful provision of nature, by which the internal world enjoyed almost perpetual light, without being subject at any time to the scorching heats which oppress the bodies and irritate the passions of the inhabitants of the external surface."

Mother Earth,
internal -

o perfect paradise!

t w o

Donald McCormick:

"One spring morning in 1884, two men stood on the banks of the river Blackwater in Essex [England] and gazed silently and admiringly at a small craft which promised them the chance of fulfilling their separate dreams and ambitions.

The elder was the owner of the craft, and already thinking of the day he would sail her in and out of the thousands of coral islands which comprise the Great Barrier Reef. The other was the man on whom the owner was pinning his hopes of making this dream come true - the seasoned seaman whom he had selected as his prospective captain."

" 'Well,' inquired the owner, 'and what do you think of her?'

His accent proclaimed him to be an Australian, and he exuded the enthusiasms of that buoyant and exuberantly extrovert nation. It was obvious from the tone of his voice that *he* thought the yacht was a veritable gem from the builder's yard, a thing of beauty and a joy to be. But the long pause before the other spoke suggested equally that he had reservations on the subject and was not quite so enthusiastic.

At last he managed to speak: 'She's certainly grand to look at and I'm thinking that she's a sturdy 'un,' he muttered cautiously. 'She needs to be. But I'm also thinking she's a titch of a craft to go to Australia under her own sail.'

Obviously the enthusiastic owner was taken aback. He seemed distinctly annoyed.

'Come, come, Captain, I expected you to say something different from that. Don't you agree she's in first-class condition?'

'Oh, her condition is all right. But she's sixteen years old, don't forget. No chicken as yawl-rigged yachts go. I warrent she's had a fair share of the sea already. A first-rate job for cruising in home waters, but a trip to Australia poses a good many problems. You hadn't thought of shipping her out as deck cargo?'

'Mr. Dudley,' replied the other testily, 'if I had, I certainly shouldn't have sent for you. I chose you from a list of many applicants for this job because I understand you have the qualities and experience for this trip.'

'It's my experience that tells me this is a risky proposition. And I've had enough experience to tell me that one thing a seaman can't tell for sure is what the weather is going to be like a thousand miles away in two months' time. We're going to need good luck and good weather for this trip, especially when we're approaching the Cape.'

'If you accept my proposition, you are absolutely free to pick your own time for making the voyage and you can stop whenever you think it's desirable.'

'There won't be many stops after Madeira, I'm thinking.'

'You couldn't make a coastal trip, hugging the shore of Africa to the Cape?'

'It would take too long and there would be just as many risks with on-shore gales. Not many worthwhile ports we could call at south of the Equator on the African coast. Fact is, what with the blackamoors and cannibals, we'd be safer off at sea.'

Both men laughed at this.

'I bet you could tell some tales of cannibals, Captain.'

'Happen I could. But that's beside the point. If I take this job on, it will have to be the quickest route on the chart - as direct a straight line as sailing will permit. Anyhow, it's a challenge and I've never funked a challenge yet. Nor shall I now.'

'Splendid! Then it's agreed that you will be skipper and find a crew as quickly as possible?'

'If I can get the crew I want, I'll accept. But they'll take some finding, sir. You see, the best sailors know too much about the sea and they don't fancy the risks of getting becalmed a thousand miles from land in a tiny yacht.'

'How many men will you require?'

'We don't want too many. First, because we couldn't carry the provisions for 'em; second, because too many sailors, like too many cooks, get in each other's way. I want a few good men, that's all. I'd settle for a mate, one able seaman and a boy.' "

"The craft of which we have been speaking was the *Mignonette*, a yawl-rigged vessel built at Brightlingsea in 1867. She was a small yacht of only nineteen tons, with a length of fifty-two feet, a beam of twelve feet one inch, and a draught of seven feet four inches. The vessel was listed in Lloyd's first *Register of Shipping* in 1878 and continued to be shown until 1884 under the ownership of Mr. Thomas Hall, of Barnard's Inn, London. But in 1882 Mr. Hall had sold her to a fellow barrister, Mr. Henry J. Want, of Sydney, New South Wales.

Mr. Want had been born in Australia in 1846 and educated partly in France. He was an able and eloquent barrister who had just embarked on a political career. Indeed, it was the prospect of politics which now made it necessary for him to hurry home ahead of the yacht he had bought.

Henry Want felt that a craft with so relatively low a draught would be ideal for cruising around the islands of the Great Barrier Reef and it was his ambition to take *Mignonette* on a summer cruise from Sydney, up the eastern coast of Australia, among the 80,000 square miles of warm, tropical seas dotted with thousands of pine-covered islands to spear turtles and hunt for the dugong. Previously his yachting had been mainly confined to short trips out from Sydney.

With this end in view he had selected Captain Thomas Dudley, then stationed at Colchester, to sail *Mignonette* from Tollesbury in Essex to Sydney. It is true that he had been warned this was a hazardous enterprise, and that the considered opinion of experts was that she should travel as deck cargo rather than under her own sail. But he felt quietly confident that a first-class seaman could carry out the operation and Dudley was a natural choice for the assignment for he came from a family of sea-faring people, his father and brothers all being sailors. He was a tall, impressive man of thirty-one, with a striking personality and a mahogany-hued face that gave evidence of many years spent at sea, and, according to his testimonials, 'a man of exemplary character', 'thoroughly dependable and trustworthy' and 'able to tackle any job requiring skilled seamanship, courageous and with real power of command.' "

"The pay for this voyage to Australia was good - well above the average, for Mr. Want was a wealthy man - and in addition the Australian had promised Dudley and the other members of the crew a substantial bonus if the yacht was delivered safely before the end of September. It was an operation not without risks, but, given luck as far as the weather was concerned, and careful seamanship, the ultimate rewards more than outweighed the disadvantages.

Want took a liking to Dudley, despite the latter's contemptuous reference to the 'titch of a craft.' He lost no time in engaging him as captain and Dudley set about finding a crew. But this, as Dudley feared, proved far from easy. Potential crew were apt to dwell upon the disadvantages rather than the financial rewards. To many the idea of being cooped up in a small craft on meagre rations for so long a voyage was somewhat of a nightmare."

"Finally the crew was completed by the signing on of Richard Parker, a seventeen-year-old boy who lived in the neighborhood of Southampton.

It was a small and young crew. Brooks, the third hand, was the eldest at thirty-eight and the mate, Edwin Stephens, was thirty-six. They were tough, seasoned men, though, with the possible exception of Parker, who had no previous experience of ocean sailing. But Parker, like Dudley, had the tradition of the sea in his family."

"Dudley had carefully chosen young Parker as being an intelligent, high-spirited and well-behaved lad, to whom the prospect of a long voyage to Australia was something of an adventure.

Mignonette completed her refitting, provisioned, and on May 19 she sailed away from Southampton, passed the Isle of Wight and out into the English Channel on the first leg of her lengthy voyage."

"For the first three weeks of their trip the weather favoured them. At times they made fifteen knots and Dudley began to feel that *Mignonette* fully justified her owner's praises.

In these early days they kept to the main trade routes and hardly a day passed without their sighting a ship, or another yacht. With the Atlantic as calm as a pond their duties were not onerous, and off watch they spent their time reading, playing poker and sun-bathing. Brooks acted as cook and occasionally added to their stock of food with some catches of fish. As they approached Madeira shoals of dolphins were frequently encountered and one shoal followed the yacht for five days. They swam astern of *Mignonette* in a precise, battle fleet formation, from shortly after dawn until just before noon; then, as though their leader had given a signal, they swiftly and in unison dived out of sight and were not seen again until late afternoon. Ostensibly the dolphins were on the look-out for flying-fish which appeared to be their favourite form of food."

" 'You should take a look at the book I've been reading,' interposed Dudley rather sternly. 'Then you might not joke about such things.'

'Oh, what's it about? Cannibals?!'

'In a way, yes,' replied Dudley. 'It's called *The Narrative of Arthur Gordon Pym*, by a chap named Edgar Allan Poe.'

The conversation changed abruptly for at that moment the isles of Madeira were sighted and Dudley ordered Stephens to make out a list of stores required."

" 'So far luck has been with us,' Dudley told the others when they put in at Funchal. 'But the real dangers lie ahead. We could stay here for four days and still be a day ahead of schedule when we leave. But I don't want to do that. Once we cross the Line we must expect storms this time of the year. We shall be going straight from summer into winter and in the South Atlantic it isn't easy to hold a course when storms blow up. We need to have five days in hand when we leave Madeira as we shall surely lag behind for a while somewhere between here and the Cape. But our first job is to stock up with sufficient stores to see us to the Cape even if we do get becalmed on the way.'

So their stay in Madeira was brief enough."

"On the morning of the day they sailed from Madeira, the crew of the *Mignonette* took a flagon of wine and some sandwiches down to one of the beaches for a picnic lunch. With the knowledge that this was to be their last visit ashore for possibly months to come they were anxious to savour every moment of it - the narrow stretch of gleaming-silver-smooth beach jutting inland like an eager tongue out of the waves, the hibiscus and bougainvillaea growing on a terrace just above them and the itinerant guitarist in the distance.

Suddenly a shriek came from the direction of the sea. Stephens pointed to a barely discernible figure frantically struggling in the Atlantic waves some fifty yards away.

'It's a girl, or a boy,' he shouted. 'In real trouble by the look of things.'

'She's in worse trouble if she loses her nerve like that,' added Brooks. 'Wonder if it is a girl.'

Dudley said nothing, but quietly took off his coat and trousers and and dashed into the water. There was quite a heavy sea running and swift cross currents; even for a strong swimmer like Dudley the attempt at rescue was extremely risky, the more so as the struggling person appeared to be in a state of panic. Dudley carved his way towards her with long, powerful overarm strokes and he was breathless himself when he reached the nearly demented figure. It was a girl, thought Dudley, though she has a boy's features. At first she resisted his efforts to keep her afloat. It took him all his time to calm her down, turn her on her back and get a firm hold of her arms just above the elbows. Dudley was skilled in life-saving, for which he held a certificate, and he knew exactly how to prevent the girl from turning around and struggling.

Even so he was almost exhausted himself when eventually he brought her ashore and gently laid the limp, unconscious figure on the beach.

'Then it is a girl,' chortled Brooks. 'What a salvage prize! She's a good looker, too, but in a queer sort of way.'

'Don't stand there joking,' retorted Dudley angrily. 'If we don't do something quickly, she'll die. Give me a hand at bringing her round.'

For several seconds Dudley feared she was dead. He placed the girl face downwards, knelt astride her and, with his fingers spread out on each side of her body over the lowest ribs, leaned forward so that his weight produced a firm downward pressure. Backwards and forwards, slowly and gently, he swung in an effort to drive the water out of her lungs. After six minutes there was still no sign of life and Stephens, who was also trained in artificial respiration, took over.

The feverish efforts of the two men, each taking it in turns of five minutes at a time, continued for what seemed hours, but was actually less than half an hour. Finally Dudley bent over the inanimate figure and pressed his lips against hers, tugging at his lungs to breathe life into her.

'She's dead,' said Stephens laconically. 'There's nothing more we can do.'

'I refuse to believe it,' replied Dudley. 'I'm going to have one more try.'

Sweating hard in the sub-tropical sun, his lungs aching with every breath he took, Dudley again pressed his lips against those of the girl. By this time a crowd had gathered on the beach and Stephens had sent one of them running to fetch a doctor.

Suddenly Dudley realized with fierce joy and pride in his heart that she was faintly breathing. He continued to massage her back until she opened her eyes and gazed around in frightened bewilderment.

'No,' she murmured in Portugese. 'It is not true. I am dead.'

'You are alive,' replied Dudley. 'You must keep telling yourself that. You are alive and safe.'

An interpreter was found among the crowd and, having questioned the onlookers, he told the English sailors that the girl was Otilia Ribeiro, a seventeen-year-old orphan from Funchal. Someone recalled that she sold flowers and had a passion for ships and the sea.

'But what was she doing so far out from shore?' asked Dudley, somewhat puzzled.

The onlookers shrugged their shoulders. When she had recovered a little, the interpreter questioned the girl closely, but she declined to reply.

'If you ask me, *senhor*, she wanted to do away with her life,' he added.

'Strange that so young and attractive a girl should want to die,' commented Dudley. 'Very strange, for surely she has much to live for.'

'She is an orphan, *senhor*, and life can be very hard for an orphan.'

'She is mad,' said another. 'She has no friends. She's in love with the sea.'

There was laughter among the crowd and Dudley inquired the reason for this.

'They say,' explained the interpreter with a smirk, 'that her *amigo* is the sea.'

'And what's so funny about that?' asked Dudley, frowning. 'Certainly she struggled hard when I tried to rescue her. She might have had both of us drowned. Still I should like to persuade her that life is worth living. There is not much point in rescuing somebody if she's going to kill herself again within a few days.'

'*Senhor*, there is not much one can do about it.'

'Well, I intend to try,' replied Dudley. 'Where does she live? We will take her home.'

After a doctor had arrived and treated her somewhat perfunctorily and brusquely demanded payment from Dudley, payment for which he, Stephens and Brooks had a whip-around, they discovered that Otilia lived by herself in a drab room in a Funchal tenement. The *concierge*, an unsympathetic old harridan, spat contemptuously when she heard of the girl's escapade.

'She is mad. Quite mad. She keeps to herself and her flower stall. She has no friends, not even a man. All she does is to talk about the sea and ships. She is always trying to sign on as a sea-cook, but nobody will listen to her. They know she is mad.'

'Hm,' said Dudley, 'she might be just as useful as young Parker, but I'm afraid the *Mignonette* is no place for a woman.'

'Then, watch your ship, captain,' advised the *concierge*. 'No doubt she will try to stow herself away in it. She has been known to do so before, but always they bring her back to land.'

They took the girl out for a drink and some food in one of the harbour-side cafes and at length she told them her story. She was the daughter of a fisherman who had been drowned; her mother had died in childbirth and she had been brought up aboard fishing vessels, often doing a man's job. She had always been treated more like a boy than a girl. After her father's death she was educated in a convent for three years. She had learned a smattering of English there and picked up some other phrases from English tourists while plying her trade as a flower-girl. She settled in Funchal to sell flowers because it was the only work she could get. But always her dream was to return to the sea and to sail round the world. She was not well-educated, but she had read a great deal, especially travel books and stories about the sea.

By a strange quirk of fate Australia was the country she most wanted to visit. She had read all about it and it sounded a new, exciting country where one could feel free and enjoy vast, open spaces. She hated being 'shut up' and in Funchal she felt a prisoner. The island was too small. She loved the sea because of its vastness; she would never feel alone at sea. Her grandfather had emigrated to Australia and he had written her letters full of the wonderful life of that then under-developed country. But, alas, her grandfather had died, so he could not help her to fulfil her wish.

So she rambled on, words tumbling out of her mouth in a wild enthusiasm that seemed so different from her despairing mood of only several hours previously. The *Mignonette* was going to Australia? *Si*? That was almost unbelievable. Never before, as far as she could remember, had a ship bound for Australia called in at Madeira. Possibly such a chance would never come again. Could *el capitan* take her? She would work hard, if he agreed. 'I can cook simple meals, I can mend sails -

you see, my fingers are proof of that work - and I can scrub decks as well as any man.'

'No,' said Dudley, finally but not unsympathetically, for he felt a certain comradeship for this girl with the call of the sea in her blood. 'I am sorry, but I can't take you. It would not be fair. One girl and four men would make big problems on a long voyage.'

'I would not worry the crew. I should just work and sleep. I do not eat much.'

Then Dudley thought of his employer. Mr. Want could do something for this girl. He had plenty of money. He might even help her to emigrate to Australia.

'But I will do something for you, Otilia, if you promise faithfully not to try to end your life again. You were trying to die in those waves, weren't you?'

She hung her head, then tossed it back proudly and said: 'I was and I wasn't. I love the sea and when I'm unhappy I always go for a swim. Maybe I felt one moment I didn't wish to live any more, but the next I was struggling to escape from death. That was when you heard me scream. Then when you came over to me I wanted to die again.'

'Then, listen to me. Here is my address when I get to Sydney - care of Mr. J. H. Want. If you still feel you would like to emigrate there, write to me and I'll see if Mr. Want, my boss, can help you.'

With the aid of the interpreter, who had cunningly insinuated himself into the party to lunch and drinks, Otilia was made to understand what might be done to help her. She burst into tears and expressed her deepest gratitude to Dudley."

" 'But the funny thing is she wasn't really what you'd call beautiful,' said Brooks. 'She was a good looker, but I wouldn't call her beautiful. More like a boy than a girl.'

'Right now I'd say she was the most beautiful girl in the world,' said Stephens. 'After all these weeks at sea, I wouldn't say no to a mermaid.'

'Women are all you two think about,' remarked Dudley. 'I must say I sometimes feel sorry I didn't bring her with us, but I'd have had a heap of trouble keeping your mauling hands off her.'

Richard Parker had said nothing during this conversation. Then, blushing somewhat, he interrupted nervously: 'You very nearly did have her, skipper, whether you liked it or not. Before she tried to drown herself she swam out to the yacht.'

'She what?' chorused the men.

'It was when you were ashore and I was on anchor watch. I caught her trying to sneak aboard and I shoved her off with a boathook.'

'Why didn't you tell me this before?' inquired Dudley.

'I thought you might be angry. Also I lost my head a bit because she had swum out quite far and I wondered afterwards whether she would reach the shore safely. You see, I hit her with the boathook.'

'You bloody young fool, you might have killed her,' said Dudley, his face white with anger.

'I only meant to carry out my instructions - to see nobody got aboard. I thought she might be a thief.'

Dudley knew that Parker was right; the lad had merely carried out his duty, even if he had been a bit officious about it. But, for some reason he could not explain, even to himself, he was bitterly resentful of Parker's action.

'You may have driven her to suicide, or to try to take her life,' he muttered reproachfully.

'Yes, sir. It's been on my conscience a long time. I kind of feel responsible for what happened. That's why I kept quiet about it.'

'I'm still not sure we were right in refusing her passage,' said Dudley. 'I only hope she doesn't try to drown herself again. She was mad keen on the sea.'

'Well,' said Stephens, 'it's the last chance we shall get of seeing a woman for some time.'"

*   *   *

"Thomas Dudley had taken a calculated risk. He had decided to leave the main sea route for ships bound for the Cape of Good Hope and instead to keep between the southeast trades and the westerly winds, in the hope of finding calmer weather in what was mid-winter in those latitudes. On June 25, however, the wind changed to north-west, and for five days the yacht was able to continue on her desired course. But on the thirtieth day of the month the wind veered around again to south-west, beginning to blow with gale force and churning up the sea so that the craft was buffeted into an uncertain, drunken puppet in the South Atlantic. Dudley's face was caked with salt, blistered and reddened by the tropical sun, which had beaten down on them relentlessly despite the storm clouds which scudded swiftly by. For the first few days of the gale the yacht had withstood the elements magnificently, calmly swinging up her bows and riding skywards with confidence while the seas swept over her. But gradually the storm had gained the mastery, causing leaks to spring and rigging to collapse. Under close-rigged canvas the yacht was rolling wildly."

from Narrative of A. Gordon Pym,
by Edgar Allan Poe
(*written some forty years earlier*):

"*It was now about one o'clock in the morning, and the wind was still blowing tremendously. The brig evidently labored much more than usual, and it became absolutely necessary that something should be done with a view of easing her in some measure.*

At almost every roll to leeward she shipped a sea . . ."

"When July 2 dawned, the gale had blown itself out and the yacht was becalmed until shortly before sunset, when a slight west-south-westerly breeze blew up. Dudley had expected the lull would be succeeded by another gale and for this reason remained on the bridge. His judgement was not at fault; by midnight the wind had increased in force, cutting the rigging with fierce blasts. The captain ordered reduced canvas.

On July 4 the storm had worsened. Great mountains of sea, topped with snow-white foam, loomed high above the tiny yacht. The situation was so bad that Dudley decided to heave-to until the storm blew itself out. All hands were summoned to take in the square-sail and place the canvas cover on the after-skylight.

By sunrise on July 5 Dudley calculated by his sextant that *Mignonette* was about 1,600 miles from the Cape of Good Hope. Her exact position was 27 degrees south, 10 west. Even if the storm abated, they were well off

the normal trade routes and far from getting
the assistance they so urgently needed."

*"The entire range of bulwarks to larboard
had been swept away as well as the caboose,
together with the jolly-boat from the counter.
The creaking and working of the mainmast,
too, gave indication that it was nearly
sprung."*

*"To add to our distress, a heavy sea, strik-
ing the brig to the windward, threw her off
several points from the wind, and, before
she could regain her position, another broke
completely over her, and hurled her full upon
her beam-ends."*

*"We had scarcely time to draw breath af-
ter the violence of this shock, when one of
the most tremendous waves I had then ever
known broke right on board of us, sweeping
the companionway clear off, bursting in the
hatchways, and filling every inch of the vessel with water."*

"The captain's plan was to remain hove-
to and to keep afloat with the aid of the sea-

anchor. But before this could be done the yacht was unexpectedly pooped. Stephens had been the first to realize their danger. It was his sudden shout which caused the others to look astern. An Everest of a wave was bearing inexorably down on them; it rushed on, its peak curling disdainfully as it advanced. For a moment it seemed to halt on the edge of the craft, towering precipitously above them. Then it struck like a blast of lightning, shattering the tiny craft to her keelson.

Dudley was flung across the bridge and the others were hurled down the decks into the stern. For a fleeting moment the yacht was perched crazily in what seemed like midair. Then, as she crashed down on the sea, there was a terrific thud which left Stephens half stunned as his head hit a bollard. *Mignonette's* starboard quarter was completely stove in and, turning slowly over, the yacht capsized."

"Our chief sufferings were now hunger and thirst, and when we looked forward to the means of relief in this respect, our hearts

sunk within us, and we were induced to re-
gret that we had escaped the less dreadful
perils of the sea."

"'I doubt if any castaways could have
been set adrift less prepared than we are,'
said Dudley. 'Two tins of turnips and no
water, and nearly 1,600 miles before we can
hope to spot land.'"

"We endeavored, however, to console our-
selves with the hope of being speedily picked
up by some vessel, and encouraged each
other to bear with fortitude the evils that
might happen."

"It was Brooks who spoke up at last:
'There may be other ships who have headed
out into the ocean to escape the storm and
are, like us, away from the trade route.'"

"The gnawing hunger which I now ex-
perienced was nearly insupportable, and I
felt myself capable of going to any lengths in
order to appease it. With my knife I cut off
a small portion of the leather trunk, and en-

deavored to eat it, but found it utterly impos-
sible to swallow a single morsel, although I
fancied that some little alleviation of my suf-
fering was obtained by chewing small pieces
of it and spitting them out."

" 'If anyone had told me I should eat raw
turtle meat, I would have said he was a liar,'
exclaimed Stephens. 'Now I just don't care.
I'm only too happy to have something to
munch away at. Just munching takes the
edge off one's hunger.' "

"Shortly after this period I fell into a state
of partial insensibility, during which the
most pleasing images floated in my imagina-
tion; such as green trees, waving meadows
of ripe grain, processions of dancing girls
. . ."

"About noon Parker declared that he saw
land off the larboard quarter, and it was with
the utmost difficulty I could restrain him
from plunging into the sea with the view of
swimming toward it. . . . Upon looking in the
direction pointed out, I could not perceive

the faintest appearance of the shore - in-
deed I was too well aware that we were
far from any land to indulge in a hope of that
nature. It was a long time, nevertheless, be-
fore I could convince Parker of his mistake.
He then burst into a flood of tears, weeping
like a child, with loud cries and sobs, for two
or three hours, when, becoming exhausted,
he fell asleep."

"'... perhaps an uninhabited island, skipper,' cried Parker, laughing uncontrollably:
he was the first to show signs of cracking up.
Seasickness and fever had taken its toll of
him."

"Parker still had delirious moments when
he dreamed of coral islands and babbled
about oranges and apples growing on trees."

"... my chief distress was for water, and
I was only prevented from taking a draught
from the sea by remembering the horrible
consequences which thus have resulted to
others who were similarly situated with our-
selves."

"On the morning of the seventeenth day Parker, crazed by thirst, failed to abide by the rule Dudley had laid down - that, twice a day, each man might gargle with sea water, provided he spat it out. Parker just lent over the side and drank in large quantities of sea water. Temporarily assuaged, he immediately fell asleep only to find within an hour or two that the salt water had made his thirst more acute and he was so ill and sick that he fell insensible."

"Parker turned suddenly toward me with an expression of countenance which made me shudder. There was about him an air of self-possession which I had not noticed in him until now, and before he opened his lips my heart told me what he would say. He proposed, in a few words, that one of us should die to preserve the existence of the others."

"When yachtsmen were entirely dependent on sail, those of them who ventured far from land not infrequently courted death by becoming becalmed for long periods. Among yachts' crews, as distinct from sailors of the Merchant Navy, there had for centuries been a tradition that in such circumstances, with no immediate prospects of rescue, or of food and drink, cannibalism was permissible."

"Then there flashed across his mind the memory of the book he had been reading, *The Narrative of Arthur Gordon Pym*, by Edgar Allan Poe. Vividly the words of Pym came back to him. Pym and others were castaways in a boat and perishing by starvation. They drew lots to determine who should be sacrificed to become food for the rest."

"He licked his sore lips nervously and almost exulted in the idea of just sucking soft, pliable, warm flesh."

"Revulsion had been changed to a wild, libidinous urge to eat human flesh."

". . . there was something almost sexual in the feeling . . ."

"*At length delay was no longer possible, and, with a heart almost bursting from my bosom, I advanced to the region of the forecastle, where my companions were awaiting me. I held out my hand with the splinters, and Peters immediately drew. He was free - his, at least, was not the shortest; and there was now another chance against my escape. I summoned up all my strength, and passed the lots to Augustus. He also drew immediately, and he also was free; and now, whether I should live or die, the chances were no more than precisely even. At this moment all the fierceness of the tiger possessed my bosom, and I felt toward my poor fellow-creature, Parker, the most intense, the most diabolical hatred. But the feeling did not last; and, at length, with a convulsive shudder and closed eyes, I held out the two remaining splinters toward him. It was fully five minutes before he could summon resolution to draw, during which period of heart-rending suspense I never once opened my eyes. Presently one of the two lots was quickly drawn from my hand. The decision was then over, yet I knew not whether it was for*

*me or against me. No one spoke, and still I
dared not satisfy myself by looking at the
splinter I held. Peters at length took me by
the hand, and I forced myself to look up,
when I immediately saw by the countenance
of Parker that I was safe, and that it was he
who had been doomed to suffer. Gasping for
breath, I fell senseless to the deck.*

*I recovered from my swoon in time to be-
hold the consummation of the tragedy in the
death of him who had been chiefly instru-
mental in bringing it about. He made no
resistence whatever, and was stabbed in the
back by Peters, when he fell instantly dead."*

" 'Richard,' he said in a voice that was
trembling with emotion, 'your time is come.'

'What? Me, sir?' replied the lad in a feeble
whisper, probably guessing that the captain
meant he was near to death, but not realizing
in what manner the end would come to him.

'Yes, my boy,' Dudley answered.

He took the pen-knife from his pocket and
with a short, sharp blow plunged it into the
side of the boy's neck. . . . The blood spurted
out and within a minute he was dead."

"I must not dwell upon the fearful repast which immediately ensued. Such things may be imagined, but words have no power to impress the mind with the exquisite horror of their reality. Let it suffice to say that, having in some measure appeased the raging thirst which consumed us by the blood of the victim, and having by common consent taken off the hands, feet, and head, throwing them together with the entrails, into the sea, we devoured the rest of the body, piecemeal . . .

" 'We caught the blood in the baler and drank it while it was warm,' he said, referring to the mate and himself. 'We then stripped the body, cut it open and took out the liver and heart and we ate the liver while it was warm.' "

"Parker's heart was put to dry in the sun."

The men urinated in their clothes, that the moisture might be absorbed back into the bodies, not wasted, and they went to the body of Parker furtively, eyes averted, or at night.

*   *   *

The German barque, *Montezuma*, bound from Rio de Janeiro to Hamburg, altered course near the island of Trinidad, in a whimsical search for mermaids. July 28, 1884, Brooks, at the tiller of the dinghy of the *Mignonette*, sighted the German barque, a speck on the horizon . . . roused Dudley and Stephens - exhausted on the boat's bottom . . . the men took oars, and with last strength rowed, until they were in turn sighted. At 24° South, 27° West, the dinghy drew to the ship's side . . . the men's eyes glazed and bright, hair and beards caked, legs and arms swollen and red . . . in the boat's bottom, undisguised, the mutilated carcass of Parker, heart and liver missing, blood stains on the boat's sides.

*   *   *

The dinghy was hoisted aboard, the bodily remains examined by ship's doctor. Wrapped in weighted canvas, with a prayer, Parker was committed to the waters. Dudley, Brooks and Stephens made slow recovery, below . . .

*   *   *

September 6, the *Montezuma* sailed into Falmouth harbor. Stephens, Brooks and Dudley, at Falmouth Police Court, before the Mayor and seven magistrates, were charged with the murder of Parker "on the high seas, within the jurisdiction of the Admiralty." Bail was denied, then, following public outcry, granted. Dudley returned to the comfort of his wife . . . she committed her life savings to her man's defense. (Years after, a memorial tablet to Richard Parker appeared at Pear Tree Churchyard, Itchen Ferry, and was annually maintained and cleaned through funds provided, furtively, by Dudley.)

*   *   *

Brooks was acquitted. But at a special trial, before the Queen's Bench Division, Dudley and Stephens - December 4 - were found guilty of murder. ". . . Lord Coleridge, without putting on the black cap, proceeded to pass sentence of death." December 10, the Home Secretary advised the Queen to suspend capital sentence "until the further significance of Her Majesty's pleasure." December 14, sentence was commuted to six months in prison, without hard labour.

*   *   *

(Later, Stephens, a morose and lonely figure, became deranged . . .)

*   *   *

Mr. Henry Want, owner of the lost *Mignonette*, returned to England, sought an interview with Dudley.

"I am as much to blame for young Parker's death as you," Want told Dudley. "You must try to feel that we are both in some measure responsible."

Want offered to pay Dudley's passage out to Australia, and those of his family as well.

"I can't think why you should dream of doing this for me," said Dudley.

"A letter came for you, addressed care of my Sydney office," Want replied. "It had a Madeira postmark and, knowing you had stopped at Madeira on the voyage, I opened it, thinking it might concern the *Mignonette*. . . . it told me how you had rescued a young girl from drowning in Madeira and I reckoned that put you right up top in my estimation."

1885, the Dudleys sailed to Australia.

*   *   *

It was Otilia Ribeiro, flower-girl from Funchal, who had written the letter opened by Want, telling again her gratitude to Dudley for saving her life, for giving her new hope and purpose, and telling that she had already begun her voyage to Australia - had booked as a cook on a ship bound for Luanda . . . the letter innocent of all knowledge of the fate of the *Mignonette*, the death of Parker, trial and conviction of Dudley . . . but filled with warm confession: that as a flower-girl she had been frail and helpless, a prey to all men, but "it is as though the sea is my father and lover. I belong to the sea. I do assure you I am in love with the sea, not with the men who sail her." Otilia's letter turned the heart and mind of Want - who had been disgusted with the wreck of the *Mignonette*, the cannibalism that followed - turned Want to Dudley, to give Dudley a new life in Australia.

*   *   *

Landed at Luanda, Otilia shipped as stewardess aboard a ship bound for Goa . . . spent time in Portuguese India, and finally (1886) to Bombay.

*   *   *

In a port near Sydney, Dudley set up as ship's chandler, and settled his family, his past buried from all save his wife Philippa, and from Want. But he still looked to the sea, and now and then set out for a short sail, alone. His sleep churned with nightmares: he would dream that Parker came back to life, and forgave him. Hurled awake, in the late night, he turned to Philippa, who urged him "to lead a Christian life", and to pray. But prayer did not bring sleep.

*   *   *

Somewhere, Otilia heard of the *Mignonette*, the death of Parker, trial of Dudley. She wrote Want, furiously defended Dudley, urged Want to do all possible for the man who had saved her life. There was little Want could do - he and Dudley could not associate, lest their names be linked - the past, through gossip, ventilated. The flower-girl from Funchal, the barrister from Sydney, corresponded, agreed tacitly that Dudley should not be told Otilia now knew his story.

In Bombay, Otilia cut her hair short, dressed as a man, passed as a sailor. As a man, she worked passage to Ceylon, then to Java, where her gender was unmasked. Once more a girl, she shipped to Sydney, where Want secured her a berth as stewardess on a friend's yacht.

But the urge to help Dudley, and the urge to once more be a man, do a man's work on the sea, joined forces in the flower-girl. She sometimes heard voices, telling her what to do, and she told Want that her plan came to her in a dream: to cut her hair short, dress as a man, secure berth as a cabin-boy - and to call on Dudley, befriend him, under the new name of *Richard Parker*. Want thought her crazy, the plan dangerous - but she urged and persuaded - and Want consented, turning a blind eye to the adventure.

*   *   *

"She prepared very carefully for her transformation into the role of Richard Parker. Her sleek, black hair was cut short; round her slender breasts she wound a tight bandage and she wore a seaman's cap at a jaunty angle. Her eyebrows were singed off and, speaking English quite fluently now, though with a foreign accent, she spent much time in low dives on the Sydney waterfront, learning and practising the jargon, the habits and recreations of sea-faring men, cursing and swaggering in an exaggerated fashion and drinking hard liquor with the rest. She was accepted as a man and that gave her the confidence to continue her masquerade. Developing a fondness for low company, she was more at ease among the roughest seamen than anyone else.

For days she watched the ship chandler's shop, partly to discover what times of the day Dudley was entirely alone, partly to make up her mind on how she should approach him. She knew there was no chance of his recognizing her unless she made herself known. Even then, panic seized her. Supposing Dudley thought she was a blackmailer and that he refused to believe she could be a woman. She had given up her job as a stewardess, cut herself off from all who had known her as a woman and secured casual work at the docks.

One day, when Dudley was alone, she walked boldly in.

'You are Thomas Dudley, aren't you?' she inquired, harshly and bluntly because, though fortified by some hard liquor, she was in reality afraid.

Dudley looked aghast at first. So at last his secret was out. Someone had tracked him down. Consternation showed in his face so that Otilia softened her voice when she spoke again.

'Please do not be afraid. I am a friend - perhaps, who knows, your best friend. Captain, I owe my very existence to you. You saved my life. Do you remember?'

'No, I'm afraid I don't,' replied Dudley curtly and with confused feelings of puzzlement and suspicion. If this was somebody come to blackmail him, it was an odd way of setting about it. And at the back of his mind he had a feeling there was something familiar about this strange visitor.

'Do you remember calling at Madeira in the yacht *Mignonette*? Do you remember rescuing a girl from drowning? I was that girl.'

'Are you mad?' asked Dudley. 'You aren't a girl.'

'Not in spirit any longer. But I am a girl and that very same girl, as I can prove to you.'

She took off her sailor's cap and pointed to her hair. 'That has all been cut off. I was Otilia Ribeiro, the girl you rescued. I have now taken the name of Richard Parker, the cabin boy who died. I want you to feel that I am that lad come back to life to pay my debt to you. You may think I'm crazy, but I was never saner. Captain, you must believe me and know that I want to help you.'

'I have never heard a madder story. I can't believe you.'

'You can't, or you won't, Captain? I swear to you that nobody except Mr. Want knows who I am, or anything about you or me. I promise I shall always keep your secret. You have nothing to fear from me as long as you live.' "

"... he sank down in a chair and put his head in his hands and wept uncontrollably.

She put an arm on his shoulder. 'If you wish for further proof, you can ask Mr. Want. Now will you admit you are Thomas Dudley?'

'There seems no point in denying it any longer. But, for my family's sake, promise me you won't talk about these things.'

'I have promised that already. Captain, you saved my life, you gave me the will to do what I always wanted, to be a seaman and to come to Australia. Always, ever since I was a girl, I wished to be free to roam the world, to sail where I wanted. In Madeira I felt in a prison. The sea was so close and yet there was no escape. The night after you arrived in Funchal I swam out to the yacht and kissed her hull. I tried to get aboard as a stowaway, but poor Parker ordered me off.'

'Why do you call yourself Richard Parker? To torment me? I suppose I can't blame you. What must you think of me?'

'Only this, Captain, that I admire your spirit and courage, that I have never forgotten you. No, I am not wishing to torment you, or to bring back terrible memories. I can't say exactly why I want to be Richard Parker, but I want you to feel that you saved my life and that, as a reward from heaven, I have taken his soul on earth. When I was in Goa and Java I learned a great deal about the way a soul can never die, but must always enter another body. Richard Parker's soul is not dead. It lives on in me. Of that I feel sure. Believe that and it may make you feel better.'

'You are a strange girl, Otilia.'

'You must not call me that. From now on I am Richard, a young sailor, looking for work. I now know quite a lot about the sea and ships. I can mend a sail, stitch canvas, lay out hawsers, splice a sword mat. In Funchal it was true I understood a fisherman's work, but since then I have learned much else as well.'

'But to me you are still the little flower-girl at Funchal. I must call you Otilia. I have often thought about you . . . When I was in *Mignonette* I sometimes wished I had allowed you to come, too. I feared you might try to end your life again.'

'Have no fear of that now, as long as you accept me as Richard Parker.'

'That is asking a lot. If only I could understand what your aim is.'

'Soon you will forget that I am Otilia.'

'But why should I? Is this some awful punishment? Why have you come to see me? My mind is all confused. You say you are Otilia Ribeiro and that you are grateful to me. You have no need to be grateful. I only did what many other men would have done. You say you will keep my secret, yet you insist on this mad pretence of being Richard Parker. What is it you really want of me?'

'I hardly know myself. I only know I want to help you and Mr. Want told me you had suffered cruelly from remorse. Then I had the idea - call it mad, if you wish - of becoming Richard Parker, of willing his lost soul into my body, of being to you a kind of brother of the sea, a ship-mate who wants you to feel that all is understood.' "

"Dudley was bitter. He felt that fate was playing him a crueller trick than ever. The incident at Funchal had always stood out in his memory as something romantic that he cherished. He was not in love with the girl, but he was in love with the idea of having been her rescuer, of having put his lips against hers and breathed life back into her. Damn it, he thought, one can't help being a bit mawkish about a thing like that. Dudley was not a sentimental man, but he felt cheated that the girl had now turned herself into a man and wanted to be regarded as such.

Otilia paused for a moment before replying. 'If Parker had lived, I can't say how I should have felt. But I do know that half of me is always a man. Oh, don't misunderstand me; I'm not a freak. In all ways physically I am like a woman. I just don't want you to be complicated by having another woman in your life. Of course I remember you as a man who has kissed my lips and and breathed life into me. Half of me cherishes that memory. But the other half clamours to be free, asks nothing of you, but to accept me as Richard Parker. If you can't accept that, then we must part and I will never see you again. If you don't like to call me Richard, then call me Ricardo. As I am, I would pass for my brother if I had one. You can tell your family that Otilia's brother came to say 'thank you'.'

'What if I still say I want to see you dressed up as a flower-girl and to call you by your own name?'

'Then, as I have said, it is the end. But if you try you can accept me as a boy. It's better that way. You have a wife and a family. You owe them a duty.' "

*   *   *

Otilia Ribeiro was a mystic, versed in eastern versions of the transmigration of souls. Otilia had died - the flower-girl who had tried to drown herself in Funchal - and Richard Parker, cabin-boy, was reborn. But Dudley was a simple man, who disliked disorder. He was proud to see again this girl whose life he had saved - but how forget that she *was* a girl, a girl whom he had kissed? His marriage to the pious Philippa was a mere formality, his job as ship's chandler a dull routine, after the sea. He did not want to fall in love with her, but . . .

But better accept her as a boy, than to see her once more disappear. By little, he found even her boyishness stirring his sex - to share a man's work, a man's life, with Ricardo . . .

He found her an old ship's life-boat, together they converted it into a small cabin-cruiser - christened her the *Sanctuary*. Following a day's work, they frequented shorefront taverns, drinking with the sailors.

Otilia lived aboard *Sanctuary*, at Wooloomooloo . . . did odd jobs for Dudley, made fishing expeditions, hauled small cargoes. On some of these trips, Dudley joined her.

Sailors in the taverns taunted her - why didn't she chase women, like the rest of them? She lost her temper, replied that she *hated* women . . . she generally avoided brawls, but the men were afraid of her - she had learned ju-jitsu, could fling a man over her head.

She memorized the seacoast, all bays and capes, could sail without charts . . .

*   *   *

1905, Henry Want died. There was a secret bequest in his will: if Ricardo Parker would become once more Otilia Ribeiro, flower-girl from Funchal, she would receive an annuity.

*   *   *

Otilia longed for an island, an island of her own, where she could settle in solitude, live simply from land and sea. As stewardess on Want's friend's yacht, she had explored the Great Barrier Reef, from New Guinea in the north, to Breaksea Spit to the south - and she had found her island: uninhabited, but with a supply of fresh water, with pisonia scrub, pandanus palms, tournefortia and casuarina - and in the luminous and prismatic coral were mackerel, snapper, tuna, bonito, coral trout, crabs, gropers, game-fish, swordfish and lobster.

She determined to settle the island, at least set up a base for trading contacts. It was a risky voyage for a craft as small as *Sanctuary* . . . she asked Dudley - would he go with her?

'It seems like tempting the fates,' he said bitterly, 'for Thomas Dudley to go sailing with Richard Parker.'

'You are happier since we met again,' she said. 'You look better, more at peace with yourself . . .'

'But it's an unnatural life,' replied Dudley heatedly. 'I'm a man and you're not. No amount of pretending will alter that. Do you think I've ever really made myself feel you're a boy? Oh, yes, at first I tried hard enough. In many ways you seemed like a boy and we could talk of the things seamen talk about. I honestly believed at first that this was the answer to my problems. I could be a faithful husband and father, stand by my family and keep you as just a friend. It seemed to work.'

'Then gradually I found myself thinking of you again as a woman. I wanted to beg you to stop this stupid game of being a boy, but I was afraid if I did you would only go away. And I knew that I couldn't bear that. I would rather have you as a friend than nothing at all. But I'm flesh and blood like you and now that we've got to know each other so well, sometimes I - well - want to see your hair grow again - to be something more than just a pal.'

'It wouldn't work, Tom,' said Otilia vehemently. 'I would just lose myself again as a woman. I should be back where I was - helpless and afraid.'

'Afraid of what?'

'Afraid of life.'

'Well, we won't talk about it again, at least not yet. But if I come with you, I must know I have your complete trust. It isn't going to be an easy voyage, for we shall have a lot of stores to take and not much freeboard. If I come, I come as skipper of *Sanctuary*? And I give the orders. Is that agreed?'

'It is agreed, because you've got to feel I trust you. But remember I'm still Ricardo.' "

"A mad urge seized Dudley.

In the night, while Otilia slept, he altered course. There was a strong offshore wind blowing and within a few hours the tiny craft was far out of sight of land. Now Dudley felt better and more in command of himself. He began to plan how this new adventure would shape itself, the adventure of persuading Otilia he was a man who wanted her love and intended somehow to win it.

When she awoke, Otilia expressed her surprise at the sudden change in the weather and the fact that they were out of sight of land.

'The going will be better further out,' said Dudley laconically. 'It's too risky close inshore in this gale.'

'But surely we needn't be so far out?'

'Oh, yes, it's quite all right. We can alter course soon and head in to leeward of Lady Elliot Island. But the gale may delay us, so we must start rationing ourselves. As from today, until we sight land again, I'm going on a strict diet - one tin of beans a day and no water.'

'But that's nonsense. It's not necessary. We have plenty of rations.'

'Maybe now, but we'll need plenty when we land. And if the gale delays us for three days as it easily may, our rations will look pretty scant.'

'But we were going to stock up again at the next port.'

'Well, we shan't do that now. Our next stop will be when we land at your island.'

'Why have you changed your mind?' asked Otilia suspiciously. 'I thought you were afraid of getting too far from the coast in *Sanctuary*.'

'You said I was captain for this trip, didn't you? You said you trusted me?'

'Why, yes, of course.'

'Then shut up and don't argue.'

He had never spoken to her like that before and Otilia was shocked and hurt. For a long time they didn't speak. When it came to meal-time Dudley handed out her normal rations and took for himself a single tin of beans. She opened her mouth to remonstrate, but he silenced her with a curt: 'No arguments. It's an order.'

Silently they ate, but Otilia no longer had any appetite. She knew that something was going on in Dudley's mind, but couldn't fathom what it was.

He handed her the water barrico, then leaned over the side and scooped up with a spoon some of the sea-water. She was horrified to see him drink it.

'Have you taken leave of your senses?' she asked, now thoroughly alarmed.

'No, I'm just being prudent. Remember I've learned a lot about how little a man can live on at sea. I didn't make that twenty-four day voyage

without finding out a good deal I didn't know before. Since then doctors have explained that sea-water need not be the menace to seamen
which we always imagined. Oh, yes, if I could re-live that twenty-four
days I should act very differently.'

'Sea-water will only make you ill and increase your thirst. It be-
comes like hard liquor. You start drinking it and you crave for it.'

'Yes, if you gulp it down in large quantities. That's what sends men
mad. But there's nourishment in the plankton in the sea and if I take
one spoonful every hour, it will be as much as I need.'

'And supposing you get ill?'

'I shall survive,' replied Dudley, 'and so will you. As long as I'm in
command I shall see you safe.' "

"For three more days and nights he maintained his diet of sea-water
and beans. It was part bravado, he admitted to himself, because, if
his courage failed him, he could always drink from the water barrico.
A pitiful fool he would look, if he did so! But somehow his self-imposed
abstinence made him feel good, even though at times hunger gnawed at
his stomach and the sea-water left his mouth with a dry, brackish taste.
He wanted to win this battle over hunger and thirst as much as he had
wanted to live when drifting in the dinghy. At least he was now able to
convince Otilia that the strong wind had thrown them off course and
that they would take much longer to reach their island, so therefore he
had been right to insist on rationing."

"For a day and a half more they sailed on, mostly in silence. Otilia was seasick and suffered so much herself that she hardly realized how ill Dudley was. Perhaps that was fortunate, mused Dudley. The fact she's ill makes me feel better."

"His fever was mounting and his tongue like a piece of leather, but he hung grimly on to the wheel, for Otilia was racked with seasickness and unable to take her trick. During a lull in the gale he heard her moaning softly, like a puppy dog in pain. Lashing the wheel into a fixed position, he left his post to take a look at her. She lay motionless with eyes shut and hands stretched across her head. To make her more comfortable Dudley pulled off the seaman's jacket and unwrapped the tight bandage of coarse canvas which was wound round the upper part of her body. She'll faint, if I don't remove it, Dudley told himself, and he marvelled how she would live in such a straight-jacket. At last the canvas was unwound and there she lay, inert, unprotesting and uncaring, a helpless bundle of femininity, despite her boyish looks, the small rounded breasts scored with the harsh imprint of the canvas."

"This was the moment he had hoped and waited for: the ending of the masquerade and the revelation of the girl who hid behind a seaman's clothing.

Dudley was delirious, but he did not care any longer. He exulted in his delirium which was now a joyous fever that pulsed through his veins. Back he went to the wheel, once again heading on the right course, supremely confident that now he was the master and that soon they would make a landfall."

"Dudley picked his way through the breaking surf and nosed the boat into the placid lagoon which lay ahead."

*   *   *

He dropped anchor, stepped ashore, stretched his legs on the beach. Otilia lay asleep in *Sanctuary*. Opening a flask of brandy, he placed it under her nose, and she stirred.

"Drink some of this," he urged.

"Why didn't you wake me sooner?"

"It was best that you slept."

Suddenly she realized the canvas bandage was gone . . . her hands rushed to her breasts.

"What have you done to me?"

"Otilia, this is how I have always wanted you to be - just as I found you in the sea off Funchal. I haven't done anything to harm you . . ."

She sobbed bitterly, tears of anger, of impotence and helplessness. She said nothing, and Dudley held her tight, pressed her head against his shoulder, as Ricardo, Richard, the boy-man in Otilia, wavered . . .

*   *   *

Otilia kept a diary: "Arrived in Paradise, February 2 . . . Tom takes charge."

For two weeks, Tom and Otilia shared their island, man and woman - slept, bathed, caught turtles, went fishing.

"If I died tomorrow, I should be content for never can I have a happier day."

The rains came, they gave up their shelter, returned to *Sanctuary*.

Then, this diary entry: "Tom promises to give up the pipe."

In the middle of the month, they set sail for the mainland - and caught the tail of a cyclone. *Sanctuary* was battered and holed, her rigging torn, leaking badly.

Sanctuary never went to sea again.

Nor did Otilia Riberio.

Nor did Thomas Dudley.

*   *   *

Dudley returned to his ship chandler's, to Philippa, his family.

Otilia left Sydney, left Dudley, went to Brisbane - became a fortune teller: "Miss Jack Tar". She wore a seaman's cap, smoked a pipe, and mixed her knowledge of the occult, of the secret cults of the East, that she had learned in India, or in Java, with her studies of the stars and signs of the Zodiac, and with her encyclopaedic knowledge, committed to memory, of the Great Barrier Reef and all its islands, of the entire eastern and southern coasts of Australia - so that sailors who drifted to her tent and crystal ball, seafarers and captains, about to set sail and seeking guidance, were astonished at her knowledge and wisdom.

*   *   *

"Tom promises to give up the pipe."

When Tom Dudley had emigrated from England, opened his shop in Australia, he had been nervous, distraught, plagued with nightmares . . . and he discovered opium. In the back room of a tavern, he put a pellet of the drug on a needle, held it in the flame of a spirit lamp until it sizzled, then plugged it into his pipe - smoked, and became calm. It was Tom's secret, unknown to Philippa, or Otilia.

When Tom and Otilia sailed on *Sanctuary* to the Great Barrier Reef, to the island she called Paradise, Tom smuggled opium and pipe aboard, smoked when she was asleep, when the wind would carry the scent from her nostrils. One night, when she slept and he smoked, he dreamed of slashing a morsel of flesh from his buttocks, bandaging himself with the canvas he had removed from her breasts, cooking the meat in the galley, and serving it to her when she woke.

Arrived at the island, she discovered his habit, discovered the opium - or he confided it - and perhaps they smoked together . . .

*   *   *

Years later, Dudley resumed his own name, made no effort to hide his past. Stories circulated that he had once eaten a boy, and he was known at times as "Cannibal Tom" . . . but it was all too long ago, no one cared.

*   *   *

1900, bubonic plague came, for the first time, to Australia. Its origin was traced to rats in the loft of Dudley's shop.

Thomas Dudley was the first man in Australia to die of the plague. His casket was towed down the Parramutta River.

*   *   *

When Tom died, Otilia took heavily to opium, became a hermit, had "visions". Many years later, she returned to Sydney. "I'm too old to tell fortunes any more. Too old and tired. I shall just sell flowers."

Miss Jack Tar, with sailor cap and pipe, flower-seller, was on the streets of Sydney - as late as 1925.

*   *   *

July 28, 1884, the German barque *Montezuma*, under Captain Simonsen, had altered course near the island of Trinidad, "in a whimsical search for mermaids" - and, so doing, had discovered the survivors of *Mignonette*.

Otilia knew this story, from Dudley - knew it was the quest for mermaids that had saved Tom.

Secretly, she had someone take a photograph of a dugong - that sea-going mammal of the Australian islands, with female breasts, now and then mistaken by sailors for a mermaid - and she secured Captain Simonsen's address. She sent the photo to him.

For years the Captain kept it in his wallet, brought it out for friends - the mammal that breathed air, but took to the sea.

BOOTH

one

London, early eighteen-hundreds, Richard Booth, advocate, established his son, Junius Brutus, as clerk in his office of law. Junius was bored, fled the law, joined a troupe of strolling players - tramping the country, eluding the sheriff, sleeping by the road, eating the vegetables thrown at them onstage.

1815, young Booth appeared at Covent Garden, was an instant success . . . played Iago, Richard III, Hamlet, Lear, Shylock, Sir Giles Overreach.

Crossed to America, 1821, played the great theaters of the Atlantic seaboard . . .

*　　*　　*

Junius Brutus Booth: "Rise early, walk or use some exercise in the open air, and, when going to bed drink a warm liquid - either weak grog, gruel, or even water; drink nearly or quite a pint at one draught. Lie down directly, and in fifteen minutes you will sink into a comfortable lethargy. Coffee and tea, however, must be avoided, as they prevent sleep. A slice of bread-and-butter, and an onion or lettuce for supper, prior to this potation, is good - much opium, and of a harmless quality, being contained in the latter vegetable."

. . . revived himself after the play with a pint of porter or a glass of brandy . . . then, a drink or two beforehand, to brace himself . . . finally, to act when drunk . . .

locked in his hotel room, before the play, he bribed a passing bellboy to bring mint juleps, which he sucked through the keyhole with a straw . . .

. . . thrown into jail in Albany by his manager, to keep him sober, he bribed the chore boy to bring brandy, which he sipped through a Shaker pipe stuck through the cell's close grating . . .

. . . walked about the streets in full costume . . .

. . . in Natchez, climbed a ladder into the flies, during Ophelia's mad scene: crowed like a rooster . . .

"I can't read! Take me to the lunatic asylum!" he shouted in Boston: was hustled offstage, simpering and screeching with laughter . . . was later seen walking to Providence in his underwear, shaking his head, gesticulating . . .

"I must cut somebody's throat today. Whom shall I take?" he demanded at rehearsal, and whipped out a dagger . . .

. . . in the duel scene in *Richard III*, he chased Richmond through the stage door and into the street . . .

. . . as Othello, nearly suffocated Desdemona with a pillow . . .

*   *   *

Age 26, Junius Brutus Booth suddenly tired of the theater, "where nothing is but what is not." He applied for the job of lighthouse keeper at Cape Hatteras . . . but his business managers, not wishing to lose so valuable a property, made sure he was turned down . . . thereby performing a great service to those who navigate the waterworld . . .

*   *   *

Booth sought solitude, bought Maryland land, with a spring of sweet water, in the wilderness of Belair . . .

. . . bought a log cabin, unpainted and unplastered, moved it to his new land, near the spring, among the oak and beech trees, at the skirts of the dense forest - and decorated the spring with granite steps and ledges.

. . . worked in the fields, grubbing the soil and sowing the seed, in his bare feet . . .

Loved all animals, believing, with Pythagoras, that Men's souls are born again in animals' bodies . . . he refused to drown the little creatures that infested his mattresses . . .

*   *   *

When a black servant died, Booth preached the sermon, and buried the remains - outside the family plot. He loved their music . . .

*   *   *

May 10, 1851 - twelfth birthday of their son, John Wilkes - Junius Brutus Booth and Mary Ann Holmes were married.

*   *   *

An infant daughter died, and Booth returned from tour, had the body disinterred and brought into the house, hoping thereby to restore the child to life . . . when his old horse died, he had Mrs. Booth lie across the creature's body, and pray . . .

*   *   *

Junius Brutus Booth died in 1852. He looked so natural the family was afraid to bury him, until assured by Physicians he was not just in a trance . . .

t w o

The Booth children grew up in Belair - the infants, on a winter evening, in wicker cradles, before the great stone fireplace . . .

The child John Wilkes ran wild through the woods, hurling himself to the ground, sniffing the earth's breath, nibbling the sweet roots and twigs. "Life is so short - and the world is so beautiful. Just to *breathe* is delicious."

The children put on theatricals, and young Johnnie stood at a window, mimicking . . . later, he studied dance, practiced elocution in the Belair woods . . .

. . . muttered to himself, frightened the servants, brandishing his Mexican saber, raving in recitations and rehearsings . . .

Was an expert marksman, went on hunting expeditions, in defiance of his father . . . could shoot through the open neck of a bottle, at some distance, and blast out the bottom . . .

Rode horseback into Belair . . . before a crowd of villagers, dropped his handkerchief to the ground, rode off, and, returning at a gallop, swept the linen gracefully into his hand . . .

At thirteen, he ran away to Baltimore, to become an actor, or an oyster pirate . . .

*   *   *

According to neighbors, the Booth family had "dirty British blood, and being mixed up with southern ideas and niggers made it dirtier" . . .

The family was disliked because they were so secretive (*theatre - self-exhibition - is the final retreat of the secretive*)

Everyone knew that John Wilkes' sister Rosalie was "a little queer" . . . and there were those around who thought that all the Booths were "cracked" . . .

*   *   *

In Baltimore there were meetings of the Blood Tubs and the Plug-Uglies . . . John Wilkes joined the Know-Nothings: to save the Southern Way of Life from the Irish . . .

*   *   *

John Wilkes Booth: ". . . he was a perfect man; his chest being full and broad, his shoulders gently sloping, and his arms as white as alabaster, but hard as marble. Over these, upon a neck which was its proper column, rose the cornice of a fine Doric head, spare at the jaws, and not anywhere over-ripe, but seamed with a nose of Roman model . . . which gave to the thoughtfully stern sweep of two direct, dark eyes, meaning to women, snare, and to men, a search warrant . . ."

". . . the lofty square forehead, and square brows were crowned with a weight of curling, jetty hair, like a rich Corinthian capital."

"His profile eagleish, and afar his countenance was haughty. He seemed full of introspections, ambitious self-examinings, eyestrides into the figure, as if it withheld him something to which he had a right."

"His coloring was unusual: the ivory pallor of his skin, the inky blackness of his densely thick hair, the heavy lids of his glowing eyes were all Oriental and they gave a touch of mystery to his face when it fell into gravity; but there was generally a flash of white teeth behind his silky mustache and a laugh in his eyes."

"He was handsome as a young god, with his clear, pale, olive complexion, classically regular features, and hair and mustache literally black as night . . ."

"John Wilkes Booth cast a spell over most men with whom he came in contact, and I believe all women without exception."

". . . ladies wrote him scented notes . . . the stage door was always blocked with silly women waiting to catch a glimpse . . ."

. . . in Albany, a young actress dashed into his room, cut his face with a dirk, then stabbed herself . . . the cause is said to have been "disappointed affection" . . .

*   *   *

According to the critics: ". . . every nerve quivers with the passion which his words give vent to . . ." ". . . the climax of the play was never given with such desperate energy . . ." ". . . Mr. Booth has far more action, more life . . ." ". . . The effect produced upon the audience was absolutely startling and bordered nearly upon the terrible . . ." ". . . J. W. Booth has that which is the grand constituent of all truly great acting, intensity . . ." ". . . Mr. Booth seems to me too energetic, too positive, earthly real and tangible . . ."

As Othello, rushing to the murdered Desdemona, his body and scimitar slammed against her - and she held her breath . . .

In Romeo's final struggle with Juliet, he sprained his thumb, tore her clothes, lifted her out of her shoes . . .

As Richard III, he leapt over the footlights, dueled Richmond down the center aisle . . . or tumbled him into the orchestra pit, dislocating his shoulder . . .

. . . stabbed himself in the armpit, bound his right arm to her side, fenced with his left . . .

. . . following the performance, he slept smothered in oysters or raw steak, to heal the bruises . . .

*   *   *

Booth may have had a liason with a Confederate spy, one Izola D'Arcy, who traveled under invented names: Oriana Collier, Eleanore St. Clare, Hero Strong, Izola Violetta . . .

He may have visited France, met a French girl, who said "he was a madman; that he arose at night in his sleep in order to converse with spirits, and that she was so afraid that she was fleeing . . ."

A Washington tavern keeper: ". . . now sometimes drank at my bar as much as a quart of brandy in less than two hours . . ." ". . . he could absorb an astonishing quantity and still retain the bearing of a gentleman . . ."

Booth: "When I want to do something that I know is wrong, or that I haven't time for, no surer way of being rid of the temptation than just to pretend it a *reality* ..."

... he had his own initials - J.W.B. - pricked in India ink, on his right hand - perhaps to help him know who he was ...

*   *   *

Spoke with a nasal quality - or with "a mongrel sound in the back of the mouth or top of the throat" ...

... hadn't the patience, as an actor, to reach deep into his lungs and diaphragm, to truly "create" the sound ... mistrusted the unreal, for fear it wouldn't become real, was too rushed - too anxious to get the meaning out ...

1865, his career was already blighted by "bronchial trouble" ...

Booth hated Lincoln, was personally offended that a man so gross and ugly could be in the White House. A clown, a gorilla, a niggerloving railsplitter . . . the big hands, gnarled and powerful, were hands that had done manual labor . . . the sparse, shaggy body, on which clothes hung loosely and seemed ill-fit, was the body of a peasant, grotesque and brutalized by toil . . .

The Vice-President, Andy Johnson, was a treacherous, traiterous Tennessee tailor . . .

*   *   *

The theater! the theater!
the final act,
to make the unreal real,

actor and character,
role and player,
interfused,

the other become his own,
his own another,

the actor in the theater
searching final measure
for the acts
of his imagination!

*   *   *

Booth: "... the country was formed for the white, not for the black man.
And looking upon *African slavery* from the same standpoint held by the
noble framers of our constitution, I, for one, have ever considered it one
of the greatest blessings (both for themselves and us) that God ever
bestowed upon a favored nation. Witness heretofore our wealth and
power; witness their elevation and enlightenment above their race
elsewhere. I have lived among it most of my life, and have seen *less*
harsh treatment from master to man than I ever beheld in the North
from father to son..."

"O, my friends, if the fearful scenes of the past four years had never
been enacted, or if what has been was a frightful dream, from which we
could now awake, with what overflowing hearts could we bless our
God..."

... waiting until it was too late, until only ragtag Confederate rem-
nants held out in Virginia, at Guinea's Station and Louisa Court House

. . . Lee had surrendered, the war, and the cause for which it was fought, were buried . . .

> ("*It may be asserted, without hesitation, that no event is so terribly well adapted to inspire the supremeness of bodily and mental distress, as is burial before death.*")

. . . when a cause is no longer supportable, it will be supported in theater . . .

*   *   *

Always, and from the beginning, the plot focussed on Ford's . . . for a time, Booth kept two horses and a buggy in a stable at the rear: Lincoln was to be kidnapped, carried to Richmond, and held a hostage . . . Samuel Arnold was to catch the President when he was thrown out of his box at the theater . . .

The sound of the gunshot that killed the President was thought to be "an introductory effect preceding some new situation in the play."

Booth leapt from box to stage, his spur catching in the presidential bunting, throwing him off balance . . . his ankle collapsed under him, the bone broken, and he hopped, no longer the graceful actor, but ugly! like a bullfrog!

. . . nevertheless crossing the full width of the stage, savoring his exit . . .

*   *   *

A poster:

THE MURDERER
Of our late beloved President, Abraham Lincoln
IS STILL AT LARGE

$50,000 REWARD

Will be paid by this Department for his apprehension. BOOTH is Five Feet 7 or 8 inches high, slender build, high forehead, black hair, black eyes, and wore a heavy black moustache, which there is some reason to believe has been shaved off.

At Dr. Mudd's: " 'Davy,' he whispered, 'ask the lady of the house to let me have some hot water and soap - and the doctor's razor, if she will. I'm going to shave off my mustache. That's one identifying mark I can get rid of easily.' "

. . . the mark of the actor . . .

Following the assassination, and before the capture, Booth was seen on a train from Reading to Pottsville; at Tamaqua; at Greensburg; at

Titusville, where he was almost lynched - all of the above being in Pennsylvania; as J. L. Chapman of Pittsfield, Mass.; in a Brooklyn saloon; on the stage of McVicker's theater in Chicago; as a railway official in Urbana, Ohio; near Point Lookout, Maryland; in Norfolk, Virginia; en route from Detroit to St. Mary's, Ontario (he was followed by a detective); 15 miles south of Baltimore; at Eastport, Maine, where he was almost lynched; concealed in an upstairs closet in Washington; walking the streets of Washington disguised as a Negro; in New York, in bed, disguised as a female.

*   *   *

Booth was cornered in the barn at Garrett's farm: the hay was fired, the flames flickered and flared - like footlights!

Beyond the glare, the audience: the attacking soldiers, and Boston Corbett, who shot him - unseen . . .

In various collections, there are more than 200 pistols "with which Lincoln was killed" - some manufactured since 1865.

Booth shot Lincoln because they had squabbled over a woman.

Lincoln's coffin in Springfield, Illinois, is empty.

Following his capture and death, Booth was sighted in hiding in Ceylon; as captain of a pirate vessel in the China seas; playing *rouge et noir* at Baden Baden; attending the opera in Vienna; driving in the Bois de Boulogne; visiting St. Peter's in Rome; on the Pelew Islands in the Pacific; in hiding in Washington; wandering in Mexico, South America, Africa, Turkey, Arabia, Italy and China; fighting in China, with great distinction, against the Taiping rebels; playing *Richard III* in an amateur dramatics club in Shanghai; performing sleight-of-hand tricks for students at the University of Tennessee; off the New Guinea coast, in a lorcha; as a theatrical preacher, with a love of theater, in Richmond and Atlanta; in delirium in Wartburg, Morgan County, Tennessee; living out his life in England; shipping on a schooner from Havana to

Nassau; running a saloon, without a license, in Glen Rose, Texas; living with the Apaches in Indian Territory; teaching school in a log schoolhouse, Bosque County, Texas; as a soldier in the army of Emperor Maximilian; on Raccoon Creek in Friendville, Kentucky; as a cabinet maker in Sewanee, Tennessee; as a mill hand in Memphis . . .

. . . as a drunken housepainter in Enid, Oklahoma: called himself John St. Helen . . . committed suicide January 13, 1903 . . . his remains were embalmed with arsenic, rented out to carnivals . . . acquired by the Jay Gould Million Dollar Spectacle, toured the Midwest for years . . . Jay Gould died September 23, 1967, and the mummy disappeared . . . one of Gould's sons, now living (1977) in Barberton, Ohio, claims an interest . . .

five

In 1858, Boston Corbett - the man who shot Booth - had castrated himself, after being approached by a prostitute. 1887, he went berserk, tried to shoot up the Kansas State Legislature. He disappeared, but was traced to Enid, Oklahoma . . .

A visitor to Greenmount Cemetery, in Baltimore:

"As I walked after an attendant along the myrtle-bordered winding path that led to the Dogwood area, there seemed to be only one living thing in the old cemetery, a large black raven which flew ahead of us, lighting on one monument after another, performing some part of a mystic ritual as it were. Its presence there was so in keeping with the occasion, so like a fitting 'prop' for the scene, that it only seemed a touch of dramatic art when it finally arrived at the Booth plot ahead of me, and perched on top of the tall marble shaft."

BIBLIOGRAPHY

POE

Asselineau, Roger - Edgar Allan Poe - Univ. of Minn. Press, Minneapolis, 1970

Bittner, William - Poe - Boston, 1962

Fagin, N. Bryllion - The Histrionic Mr. Poe - Johns Hopkins Press, Baltimore, 1949

Harrison, James A., editor - The Works of Edgar Allan Poe - 17 vols., New York, 1902

Hoffman, Daniel - Poe, Poe, Poe, Poe, Poe, Poe, Poe - Garden City, 1973

Kaplan, Sydney - "Introduction" to The Narrative of Arthur Gordon Pym - New York, 1960

Krutch, Joseph Wood - Edgar Allan Poe; A Study in Genius - New York, 1965

Lawrence, D. H. - Edgar Allan Poe - in Studies in Classic American Literature - Garden City, 1953

Miller, Perry - The Raven and The Whale - New York, 1956

Mottram, Eric - Poe's *Pym* and the American Social Imagination - in Artful Thunder, edited by Robert J. DeMott and Sanford E. Marovitz - Kent, Ohio, 1975

Ostram, John Ward, editor - The Letters of Edgar Allan Poe - Cambridge, Mass., 1948

———— - *Supplement to The Letters of Poe - American Literature*, XXIV (1952), 358–366

———— - Second Supplement to *The Letters of Poe - American Literature*, XXIX (1957), 79–86

Poe, Edgar Allan - The Works of Edgar Allan Poe - "The Richmond Edition," New York, no date

Quinn, Arthur Hobson - Edgar Allan Poe - New York, 1969

Southern Literary Messenger, II, April, 1836, pages 336–339

Stein, Gertrude - Four in America - New Haven, 1947

Wagenknecht, Edward - Edgar Allan Poe, The Man Behind the Legend - New York, 1963

Wilbur, Richard - The House of Poe - in Poe, A Collection of Critical Essays, edited by Robert Regan - Englewood Cliffs, 1967

Williams, William Carlos - Edgar Allan Poe - in In The American Grain - Norfolk, Conn., 1925

Winwar, Frances - The Haunted Palace - New York, 1959

WATERWORLD

Dary, David A. - The Buffalo Book - New York, 1974

Gifford, Barry, editor - The Portable Curtis: Selected Writings of Edward S. Curtis - Berkeley, 1976

McCormick, Donald - Blood on the Sea - London, 1962

Seaborn, Adam - Symzonia: A Voyage of Discovery - Scholars' Facsimiles & Reprints, Gainesville, Fla., 1965

BOOTH

Bryan, George S. - The Great American Myth - New York, 1940

Clarke, Asia Booth - The Unlocked Book, A Memoir of John Wilkes Booth - New York, 1938

DeWitt, David M. - The Assassination of Abraham Lincoln - New York, 1909

Ferguson, Wm. J. - I Saw Booth Shoot Lincoln - New York, 1930

Forrester, I. L. - This One Mad Act - Boston, 1937

Grossman, E. B. - Edwin Booth - London, 1894

Jones, Thomas A. - J. Wilkes Booth - Chicago, 1893

Kimmel, Stanley - The Mad Booths of Maryland - Indianapolis & New York, 1940

Lewis, Lloyd - Myths After Lincoln - New York, 1929

Mahoney, Ella V. - Sketches of Tudor Hall and the Booth family - Belair, 1925

Ruggles, Eleanor - Prince of Players - New York, 1953

Skinner, Otis - Last Tragedian - New York, 1939

Stern, Philip Van Doren - The Man Who Killed Lincoln - New York, 1939

Weichmann, Louis J. - A True History of the Assassination of Abraham Lincoln and of 1865 - New York, 1975

Wilson, Francis - John Wilkes Booth - Boston & New York, 1929

The Jargon Society
wishes to thank the following
who are among patrons to this edition:

MARTIN S. ACKERMAN, New York City
DONALD B. ANDERSON, Roswell
DR. SHELLEY M. BROWN, New York City
D.D.C. CHAMBERS, Toronto
GUY DAVENPORT, Lexington
MR. & MRS. W. H. FERRY, Scarsdale
LLOYD R. GAG, Lemoore
BARNEY HOLLAND, Fort Worth
DR. LEVERETT T. SMITH JR., Rocky Mount
MR. & MRS. THEODORE WILENTZ, Chevy Chase